APPLIQUE DESIGNS

My Mother Taught Me To Sew

Faye Anderson

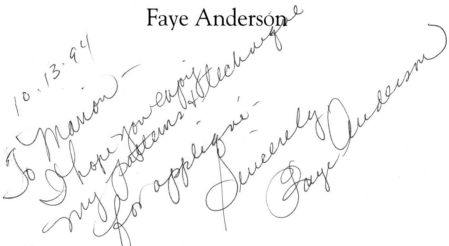

Full-Size Patterns and Instructions For Fifty Blocks

American Quilter's Society
P.O. Box 3290
Paducah, KY 42002-3290

Cover: "My Mother Taught Me To Sew," 82" x 95," © Faye Anderson, 1988
(Collection of the Artist). Photo by Jerry De Felice.

Printed by IMAGE GRAPHICS, INC., Paducah, Kentucky

APPLIQUE DESIGNS

My Mother Taught Me To Sew

Faye Anderson

The patterns for many of these blocks can be found in the pattern section, which begins on page 27.

Dedication

MY MOTHER TAUGHT ME TO SEW was created to show my gratitude to my mother, Florence Anderson for teaching me to sew and introducing me to years of pleasant hours spent with needle and thread. It is my hope that this book will introduce others to similar pleasures.

Table of Contents

Introduction

My mother taught me to sew when I was only about five years old. Hemming dish towels and embroidering pillow cases weren't necessarily very stimulating entertainments for a little girl, but they were great for developing motor skills, patience and pride in workmanship. As I watched my mother sew coats, dresses and even doll clothes with couturier expertise, being able to sew well became a goal I prized.

As a teacher my mother always required my best effort. Sloppy work and unfinished projects were definitely not allowed! But she was also patient and encouraging; she was always ready to buy fabrics for any garment I wanted to make, without being critical of my choices. As I think of the tailored blazer I once made of upholstery-weight, olive-green Indianhead cotton which was printed with huge red and black Model T Fords, I realize she must have bitten her tongue many times.

Despite occasional disastrous experiments, I was hooked right from the start on textiles and the magical process of taking yard goods from a bolt and giving them new form and function using scissors, needle, and thread.

There was no tradition of quilting in my family, so it wasn't until I was 35 years old that I discovered I could make my own unique fabric by sewing bits and pieces of cloth together into patchwork. What a revelation that was – and has continued to be! There still appears to be no end to the creative possibilities.

MY MOTHER TAUGHT ME TO SEW was inspired by a piece made by Hannah Riddle of Woolrich, Maine, in 1870. In her quilt, hundreds of small, brightly colored felt cut-outs were sewn onto a backing fabric in dense clusters.

Using traditional motifs like hearts, flowers, baskets and hands, I juggled and doodled to come up with the block designs for my own quilt. For the next two years, designing and sewing the 6" x 6" blocks provided me with my carry-along work for plane trips and travel delays.

Included in this book are pattern-layout guides for 50 of the blocks I used in MY MOTHER TAUGHT ME TO SEW, along with general instructions for construction. The techniques described include needle turn applique (which requires no basting or other preliminary work) and the use of an overlay for positioning (which eliminates the need for marking designs on the background fabric).

The blocks in my quilt – and their patterns in this book – are only six inches square, which makes some of the pieces tiny and frustrating to work with at first. To get started, you might want to read through the instructions and then enlarge one of the simpler blocks to 12" x 12" on a duplicating machine and work in that scale until you become accustomed to the equipment and techniques.

Since sewing machines make it possible for us to complete necessary sewing tasks with great speed, sewing by hand should always be a labor of love, a retreat from daily pressures. Be sure to relax and enjoy learning and practicing the techniques described!

Embroidered and appliqued signature block from the back of *My Mother Taught Me To Sew.*

Getting Started

This book contains full-size drawings of 50 of the blocks in MY MOTHER TAUGHT ME TO SEW. You can use the blocks for all sorts of projects, selecting only one or two designs or using many of them in a larger work.

In my quilt I used many of the blocks twice, repeating them in different colors. After completing the large quilt, a few more designs occurred to me so I included them in the wall quilt FLORADORA. The photographs of this wall quilt and other garments and pillow tops which are included in this book may give you ideas for your own projects using the block designs. See below and pages 78 and 79.

Once you have decided what project you plan to undertake, read through the preparation and instruction sections and then turn to the patterns to select the blocks you will use. Then you will be set to begin! The instructions are given in short sections with headings so that you can easily refer back to them as you work on your project.

One of the author's wallhangings which incorporates these six-inch appliqued blocks.

Supplies

Supplies available at art or drafting supply stores:

Lead pencil (#2)
Prismacolor pencil (#938/white)
Pencil sharpener
Circle template
18" ruler
Scissors for cutting paper or template plastic
White drafting tape
Heavy tracing paper (Bienfang 150H Satin Design)
    or Template plastic (See "Templates," pg. 11.)
Regular weight tracing paper (not dressmaker's car-
    bon)

Supplies available at sewing/quilting stores:

Scissors for cutting fabric
4"-5" EXTRA SHARP scissors
5" embroidery hoop
Thimble
Fine, sharp pins
Hand sewing needle, #8 sharp

Supplies available at hardware/building supply stores:

Materials to make a Friction Board:
    (A piece of Masonite with a piece of emery
    paper – rough side up – glued to the smooth
    side. Emery paper is a very fine grained sand
    paper.)
Materials to make a Lapboard:
    (A lightweight, rigid board with a slick, smooth-
    surface sized between 12" x 12" and 18" x 18".
    Lucite is ideal.)

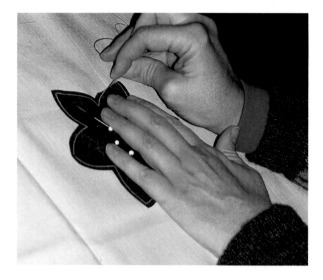

**Faye demonstrating the way she works
using a lapboard to keep the applique flat.**

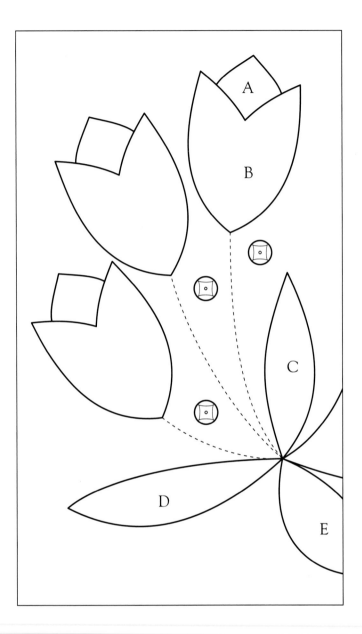

Detail of the pattern for Block Design #37 (See page 64).

Overlays

A transparent overlay is used to position applique pieces on the background before they are sewn in place. You will need to prepare an overlay for each block design you will be using. To make each overlay, cut out a 6" x 6" square of regular weight tracing paper. There is a 6" x 6" square on page 26 which you can use as a guide.

Put the square on top of the block design you want to use from this book and secure it in place with two small pieces of drafting tape. Drafting tape will stick to paper or fabric but can be picked up and repositioned several times without leaving a residue of adhesive on the fabric or tearing the paper. Using tape will aid in making the tracing as accurate as possible.

Using a sharp pencil, copy the entire design onto the paper overlay. The use of an overlay for positioning the pieces developed from my college training in graphic design. With this method, numerous small pieces can be placed precisely, one at a time as the work progresses. There is no need for marking the design on the background fabric or for trying to position the pieces with a ruler.

Templates

Each lettered shape in a design requires a template. When a shape is repeated in the design, only one template of the shape is required. Using heavy tracing paper or template plastic, trace each shape precisely and cut it out on the marked line. Place the shape on the drawing in the book to check for accuracy. Smooth any rough curves. Heavy tracing paper is easier to cut than plastic and you may wish to try both and decide which you prefer for these small templates.

You will also need to prepare a 6" x 6" template for preparation of the background fabric. You can easily do that by carefully tracing the 6" x 6" square on page 26 of this book. Cut the square out of your heavy tracing paper or template plastic and then place the template over the square you traced to check for accuracy.

Fabrics

All of the fabrics should be first quality 100% cottons and the weave should be tight and even. Coarse and irregular threads within the weave are difficult to turn under and may fray. Polyester fibers in blends remain straight instead of turning under with ease and should therefore be avoided.

The appliques require very little fabric; one-quarter yard of each will usually be sufficient! However, try not to settle for using scraps from past projects. They are too likely to be in an assortment of weaves and fibers. Take the time to find a complete palette of fabrics of similar fiber, weave, and weight, preparing them carefully before sewing. This effort will be very apparent in your finished work!

Since the designs are all small and contain many pieces, the blocks will tend to become too busy if many colors are used in each block. It's best to select one green and one or two colors for the hearts and flowers, then carefully add fabrics which are slightly lighter and slightly darker than the original pieces.

It is important for you to be able to see a marked line on the fabric (generally a white line), so avoid high contrast prints like calicoes. Two-tone prints (i.e. navy and medium blue or brown on tan) add pattern and texture to the appliqued pieces, and a marked line will be easily distinguished on them. Thin stripes and small plaids can also be used effectively.

The background fabric should be a solid color. If you choose a dark fabric for the ground, you may have to line some of the lighter appliques (See "Shadowing and Lining," page 23).

The blocks will be worked in groups of four (four blocks, equal one unit) for ease in handling while sewing and to ensure a large enough surface for use in an embroidery hoop. It doesn't matter which four you create together because after all four blocks are completed, the unit will be cut apart (with seam allowances) and the blocks rearranged for the most pleasing balance of shape and color before they are sewn together for the finished project.

Each unit (of four blocks) requires one 18" x 18" square of fabric. Decide how many blocks you wish to make and divide the number by four in order to determine the number of units you will make and therefore, the number of 18" x 18" squares of background fabric you will need.

Wash all fabrics before using them to remove sizing or glazing and to prevent future shrinkage. Use a spray-mist bottle and steam iron to remove all wrinkles.

Background Units

Remove the selvage from the background fabric and tear on grain into 18" strips. Tear the strips into 18" squares. Fold each square diagonally to see if it is truly square. Stretch opposite corner until it is true (Fig. 1).

With a steam iron, press the block and tame the edges if they have rippled in the tearing process. Overcast the four edges with a machine zigzag or turn under a narrow hem and straight stitch all around to prevent fraying while handling.

Fold the square into quarters, finger pressing each side about 1" in from the edge (Fig. 2). Measure and mark 1" on each side of the fold on all four sides and lightly mark a line from top to bottom with a lead pencil (or white pencil if you are using a dark background fabric). If you plan to wash your completed units, these lines may be drawn with a water soluble disappearing ink pen, following the manufacturer's directions.

Use the plastic or heavy tracing paper template you prepared earlier for a 6" x 6" square to complete your markings. Place the template in each quarter of the background fabric square to draw the remaining two sides of each 6" x 6" block outline.

Each block will be worked within a 6" x 6" block outline.

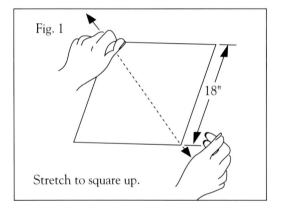

Fig. 1

18"

Stretch to square up.

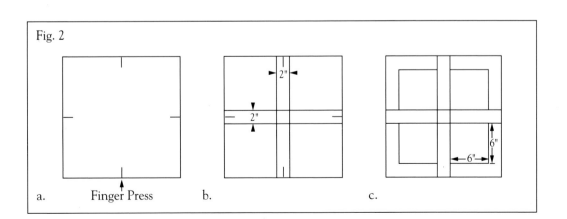

Fig. 2

a. Finger Press   b.   2"   2"   c.   6"   6"

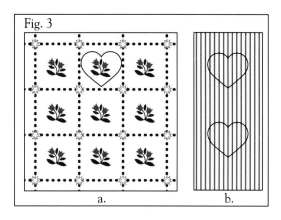

Fig. 3

a.　　　　b.

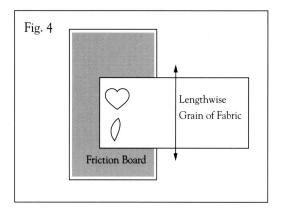

Fig. 4

Lengthwise
Grain of Fabric

Friction Board

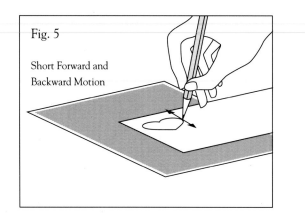

Fig. 5

Short Forward and
Backward Motion

Selecting Fabrics

Select fabric for each of the pattern pieces in your block. Put the clear plastic or transparent paper template on several fabrics to see how the size and shape of the template relate to the print of the fabric. Perhaps you can center a template over a flower to frame it, or on a stripe for a radiant effect (Fig. 3).

Don't try to use all of your fabrics in each block. The pieces are small and each color needs to be repeated to make any impact. The finished project will be more attractive if there has been some color-pattern repetition within each individual block. You may wish to cut some of the shapes out of several fabrics before deciding which would look the best.

Marking

To accurately transfer each template shape to fabric, use a friction board to prevent the fabric from shifting as it is being marked (Fig. 4). Place the fabric right-side up on the friction board and position the template on the lengthwise grain at least ¼" from the edge of the fabric.

Holding the template firmly in place, use a sharp white pencil (held perpendicular to the board) to mark around the template with short, forward and backward strokes to make a bright, crisp line (Fig. 5). If white will not show on your fabric, a hard lead pencil may be used. White, however, is preferred because the carbon from the marking will be picked up on the needle and thread and leave a sooty edge on the applique. Sharpen the pencil frequently because the lead is soft and will dull quickly.

For speed and accuracy it is worthwhile to buy an engineer's or draftsman's circle template (circles in graduated sizes cut out of a square sheet of heavy plastic) instead of cutting templates for the many sizes of circles used in the block designs. Use the circle that is slightly larger than the one on the pattern because you will be tracing around the INSIDE of the template, slightly decreasing the finished size. Use a very sharp pencil and the friction board.

Cutting

Cut out each piece, allowing a ³⁄₁₆" seam allowance. To get an idea of what ³⁄₁₆" looks like, use a ruler to mark the allowance around the first piece you cut. This should help you visually approximate this amount on other pieces without measuring.

Three-sixteenths may seem an odd number, but for the size of the appliques in these blocks, ¼" is too large a seam allowance to turn under and ⅛" is too small and may fray. After you have sewn a few pieces you will see that ³⁄₁₆" is the most manageable size for work in this scale.

Note: Some pieces in patterns #42, 44 and 47 need to be cut with the Cut-As-You-Go method. (See "Cut-As-You-Go," pg. 22.)

Clipping

The applique pieces will be positioned one at a time, in order to avoid having extra pins on the block that could catch the sewing thread as it is drawn through for each stitch. Before a piece is positioned, its inside points and inside curves need to be clipped (Fig. 6). With small, extra sharp scissors carefully snip the seam allowance all the way to the marked pencil line on any concave curve or inside point (i.e. the top of a heart). Note: Inside angles should not be clipped until you are sewing ½" from the angle. Tight curves will require more snips, close together. The snips can be further apart on gentler curves. Do not clip outside (convex) curves or straight lines because they do not require easing.

Note: Patterns #42, 44 and 47 are clipped using the Cut-As-You-Go techniques described later.

Positioning

Place the tracing paper overlay on one of the squares marked on the background fabric, carefully matching the four corners (Fig. 7). Secure in place along the top edge with a 2-3" piece of drafting tape. Slip applique piece "A" under the tracing and move it around until it is perfectly aligned. Then flip back the overlay and pin the piece in place. Two pins, one on each side of the applique, will prevent shifting. The smallest circles will need only one, and the larger motifs will need more. Do not pick the work up to place the pins; slide them in, holding the work flat against the table or board it is lying on. Once the pins are in place, flip the overlay down and check to see that the pinning hasn't caused the piece to shift. When the piece is correctly in place, remove the overlay.

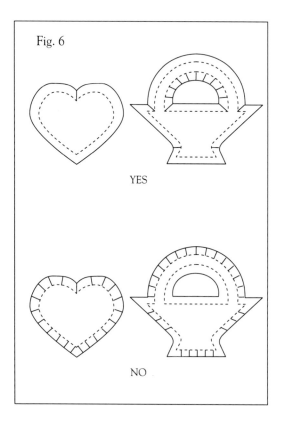

Fig. 6

YES

NO

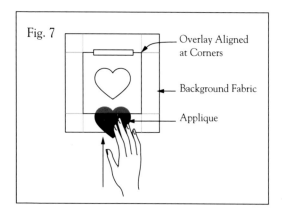

Fig. 7

Overlay Aligned at Corners

Background Fabric

Applique

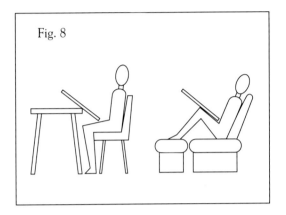

Fig. 8

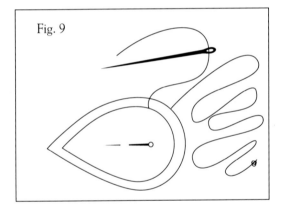

Fig. 9

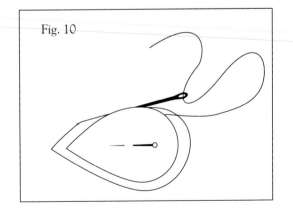

Fig. 10

Sewing

The needle used for sewing must be long so you can use it to maneuver the fabric. Quilting needles are too short and will be a handicap. High quality (very sharp) #8 Sharps are ideal because they are long and thin and will not leave holes in fine, tightly woven fabric. Select thread to match your applique. If there are a number of colors in the fabric and one color of thread will not blend in with all of them, you can use thread that matches the background fabric.

Another essential tool is your lapboard. I began using a lapboard because I wanted my applique to be accurate and to lie as flat as if the designs had been printed on the background. Holding the work in my hands seemed to create many problems. It caused eye strain because I unconsciously brought it closer and closer to my face the longer I worked, it caused the piece to conform to the shape of my finger tips, and it also took its toll on fabrics. A piece that began crisp and smooth would become droopy and lumpy and worn looking. When I began using a lapboard, everything improved.

Sometimes I sit at a table with the board resting on my lap, angled against a table. More often I am in an easy chair with my feet propped on a footstool at a comfortable angle, resting the board in my lap. Either way, the work remains flat on the board as I work, and is picked up only for the first and last stitches on each applique.

Place the lapboard comfortably on your lap or on an angle against the edge of a table (Fig. 8). Put your work flat on the lapboard. Always position a piece on your lapboard so that you will work on the top edge of it. If you are right-handed, you will work counterclockwise; if you are left-handed, you will work clockwise.

Using about 18" of thread with a single knot on the end, bring the needle through from the back of the applique piece along the marked line (Fig. 9). With the knot concealed on the back of the applique, fold over the seam allowance and make a small stitch to anchor the work to the ground fabric. About ½" ahead of the anchor stitch, place the needle in on the marked line of the applique, pull the fabric slightly forward and use the needle as an edge to fold the seam allowance over with the thumb and index finger of the other hand, creasing lightly (Fig. 10).

While still holding the crease, slide the needle out and place the applique onto the background. Put the needle into the ground fabric directly to the side of where the thread is coming out of the applique. The needle should travel in a straight line on the back side of the work and emerge about ⅛" to ³⁄₁₆" ahead and catch only a thread or two on the edge of the applique when brought back to the surface. Use the side of your thimble (worn on the middle finger) to push the needle through, all the way to the eye. Developing dexterity with your needle and thimble will take practice, but they do make the work easier – don't become discouraged! Be sure to use a thimble that fits properly and has dimples that are deep enough to catch and securely hold the needle as it is pushed through the materials.

Bring the needle straight out until the thread is taut. After several stitches eliminate bumps and puckers by running your index finger over the stitches in the direction you have been working, to smooth the edge of the applique and loosen the thread slightly if the tension is too tight (Fig. 11). Stitch the area that you have folded and finger pressed (usually 2 or 3 stitches) then advance, repeating the process of placing the needle through the applique and using it as an edge to turn back the seam allowance along the marked line.

Stitches should be between ⅛" and ³⁄₁₆" apart on the surface. For very tight curves, the stitches will need to be closer together to secure the line of the curve. Straight lines do not need to be worked so closely. The stitches should be nearly invisible on the surface and on the back they should be the same length. They should also run in a straight line, echoing the shape of the applique, with only the slightest break where the thread has gone to the surface to catch the applique edge (Fig. 12). If they look like chicken tracks that zig and zag, the thread is advancing between the layers of fabric instead of moving forward only on the back of the work (Fig. 13).

Keeping the work flat on the lapboard will prevent puckering. If you hold the work in your hand, the tension of the stitches will make the fabric form to the shape of your fingers (Fig. 14).

Holding the fabric tightly will also shift and stretch the applique out of shape.

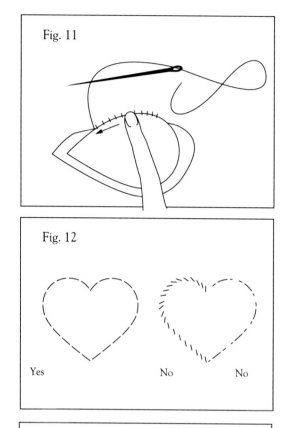

Fig. 11

Fig. 12

Yes   No   No

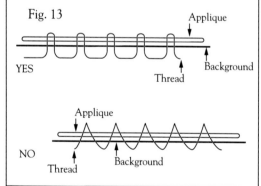

Fig. 13

Applique

YES   Background
          Thread

Applique

NO   Background
Thread

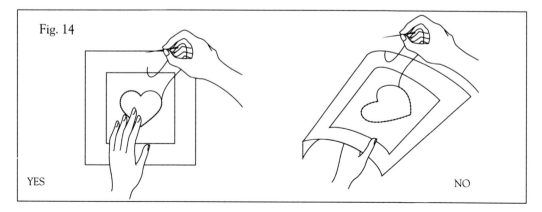

Fig. 14

YES   NO

17

Curves

An appealing feature of designing with applique is the wide range of motifs and shapes that can be incorporated. It is possible to use delicate curvilinear and organic forms that cannot be achieved in piecework. Therefore, along with having nearly invisible stitches, you should strive to have flowing, smooth curves without awkward breaks or joints.

First, it is important that you have marked your applique with a fine, crisp line. If the line is not easy to see, you will not be able to turn back the seam allowance precisely. The line must be very sharp and the edge turned under until it disappears, and no further. In general, most applique work is in a larger scale than the pieces that are in these blocks, and for larger pieces the exactness is not as critical. With small pieces, a wobbly edge can change a flower into a nondescript blob.

After you've finished sewing around a piece, make a single knot on the back side; then make two tiny back stitches next to the knot on the back side of the applique and bury the tail of the thread before snipping (Fig. 15). This is especially important if you have a light color background fabric and do not want dark thread tails to show through to the front.

There are two tricks for smooth curves which can be done AFTER the stitching has been completed. First, feel the edges of the piece you have sewn. Where you feel, or can see that there are lumps, slip the tip of the needle under the folded edge of the applique. Your needle will be between the applique's folded-under seam allowance and the background fabric. Ease out the bunching that has created the lump (Fig. 16). Work it out from either side of the lump. Do this all the way around the applique until the curve is consistent and smooth.

If there are flat areas where there should be a fuller curve, you can fill out the curve by slipping your needle tip into the fold behind the flat area and gently pushing outward in the fold (Fig. 17). This will add a little extra fullness between the stitches. A minute or so spent making these fine adjustments on each completed applique is really worthwhile. As you work with these techniques, your curves will become smoother and smoother – so be patient with yourself.

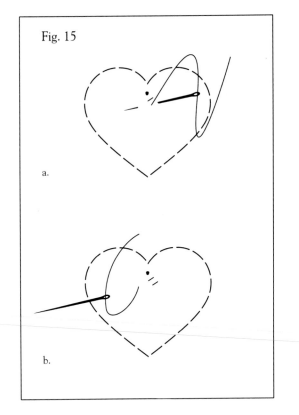

Fig. 15

a.

b.

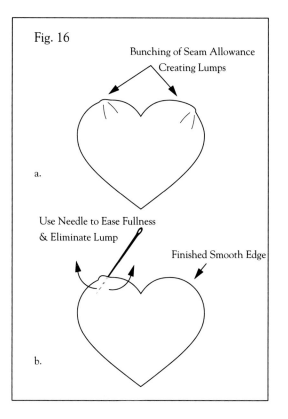

Fig. 16

Bunching of Seam Allowance
Creating Lumps

a.

Use Needle to Ease Fullness
& Eliminate Lump

Finished Smooth Edge

b.

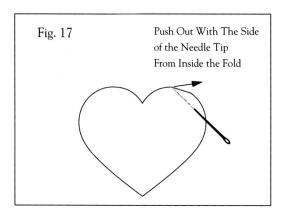

Fig. 17

Push Out With The Side
of the Needle Tip
From Inside the Fold

Points

There are two types of points in applique work, double-fold and triple-fold. The double-fold is used for points that are 90 degrees or more, the triple-fold for points that are less than 90 degrees. For the double-fold, you stitch to the very end of the point and then take a second tiny stitch in the same spot to anchor the piece. Turn your work to keep the edge of the applique you are working on at the top of your board so that you can work horizontally. Use the side of the needle as an edge to fold over the remaining seam allowance. Then continue stitching (Fig. 18).

The triple-fold is for sharper, narrow points and requires some practice. Trim the seam allowance the same as any other piece. Do not cut off the tip or trim more closely than you would elsewhere. Stitch to within ½" of the point, fold under the seam allowance at the tip and then between the last stitch and the tip. Finger press and continue to stitch to the tip (Fig. 19). When you reach the tip, take a second tiny stitch to anchor the point, turn the work and flip under the opposite side using the side of the needle to fold over. Sometimes a knob may develop instead of a sharp point (Fig. 20). This can be avoided by 1) using only good quality, fine, even-weave cottons, 2) leaving enough seam allowance so the folds can be made neatly and you won't have to poke ragged threads under, and 3) always using a triple-fold for narrow points – a double-fold will not work. Overhandling can cause the fabric to twist out of shape and cause points to droop in the direction you are stitching (Fig. 21). Handle the fabric lightly, keeping the fabric grain straight.

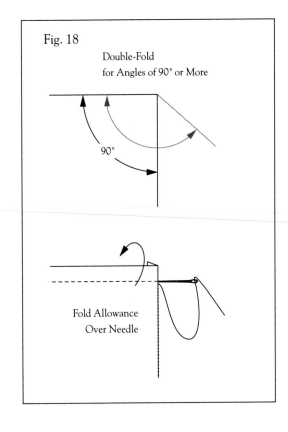

Fig. 18

Double-Fold
for Angles of 90° or More

90°

Fold Allowance
Over Needle

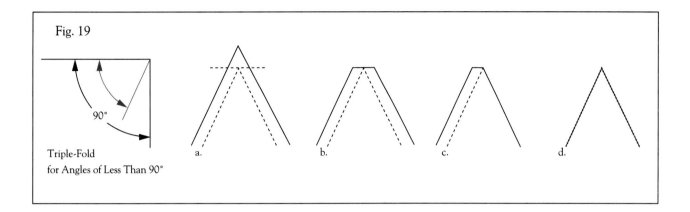

Fig. 19

90°

Triple-Fold
for Angles of Less Than 90°

a.

b.

c.

d.

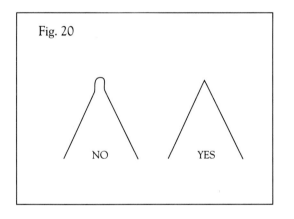

Fig. 20

NO

YES

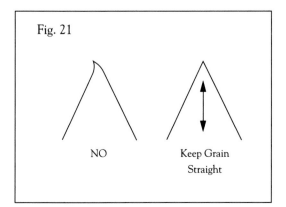

Fig. 21

NO

Keep Grain
Straight

Fig. 22

a.

b.

Inside Angles

It is essential to have very sharp, small scissors when clipping inside angles. Large shears or dull blades will chew the threads and make an unruly mess in these delicate spots. You will need to cut cleanly to the marked line, cutting through even the last thread, which will have lead showing. Be brave! This cannot be done halfway, or haphazardly. Do not do this until you are about ½" from the angle to avoid fraying while handling. Do not try to fold the seam allowance in this area over the needle. Instead, use the tip of the needle to sweep it under in one motion, then stitch to the base and take two tiny overcast stitches to secure (Fig. 22).

Cut-As-You-Go

Patterns #42, 44 and 47 contain ornate shapes that may fray or stretch if all the seam allowance is trimmed before you start sewing. For these pieces, cut away the fabric in only a small section immediately ahead of where you are sewing, doing the trimming and necessary snipping step-by-step as you progress around the applique (Fig. 23).

Trimming

There are several block designs which have layered pieces (appliques on top of appliques). To avoid bulk and eliminate extra layers that would be difficult to quilt through, these must be trimmed. After sewing the first piece on, press lightly with an iron from the back side. Then trim away the background fabric underneath the piece to within ¼" of the stitching. On the front, position and stitch the next piece on top of the first. Press from the back side then trim again, and continue the process (Fig. 24).

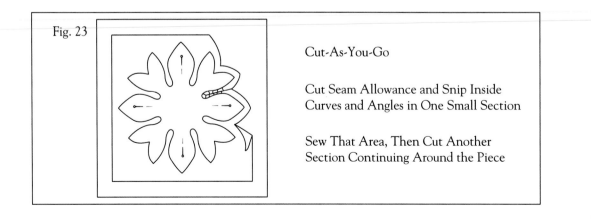

Fig. 23

Cut-As-You-Go

Cut Seam Allowance and Snip Inside
Curves and Angles in One Small Section

Sew That Area, Then Cut Another
Section Continuing Around the Piece

Shadowing and Lining

Background fabrics that are medium to dark in color may show through appliques that are light in color. This is called shadowing and will detract from the finished work. To tell whether a fabric will shadow or not, fold under an edge and lay it on the background fabric. If a line is visible where the double thickness ends, pieces cut from this fabric should be lined. If the fabric is a solid color, lining fabric can be the same as what is being used for the applique. For print appliques, use white or ivory cotton for the lining.

Trace each template twice, once for the applique and once for the lining. Cut out the applique with the usual ³⁄₁₆" seam allowance. Cut out the lining one thread inside the marked line, leaving NO seam allowance (Fig. 25). Hold the applique up to a light. Put the lining behind the applique and align the two pieces with the aid of the shadow. When the lining is exactly inside the stitch lines of the applique, pin the two together. Position this double-layered piece under the paper overlay as you would any other applique. Use enough pins to keep the lining from shifting during sewing. Having the lining edge to turn the applique seam allowance over will make the turning and sewing progress more easily and quickly.

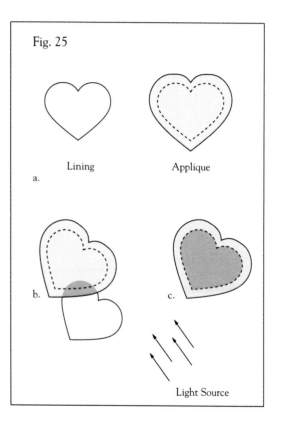

Fig. 25

a. Lining   Applique

b.   c.

Light Source

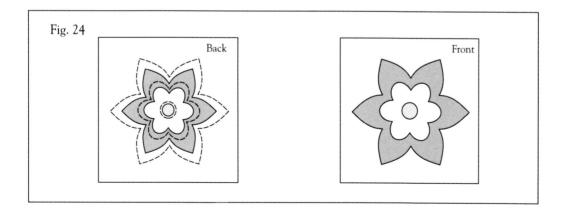

Fig. 24

Back   Front

Embroidery

Use a ruler to measure and draw the straight lines to mark your blocks for embroidery. You may sketch the curved lines in freehand, use dressmaker's carbon and a tracing wheel or trace them on a light table or against a bright window. Disappearing ink, white or lead pencil can be used. The embroidery can be done with either a stem stitch or a chain stitch (Fig. 26). Use good quality floss for best results. Remove two strands from six-strand floss. Separate these two strands, let them dangle freely to relax and straighten, and then put the two together again. Run your fingers the length of the strands, thread the needle and securely knot one end.

This process will help keep the strands from becoming twisted as you sew. The stitches will lie flatter and the smooth strands will reflect light and be more lustrous. If they become twisted while you work, turn the work over and let the needle and thread dangle freely and untwist before continuing. Stitches should be about ⅛" long. When turning a corner, sink the thread to the back side and make a single knot before changing stitching direction on the top surface. Bury the tails in the areas behind applique whenever possible (Fig. 27). Use a small embroidery hoop (appoximately 5") for proper tension.

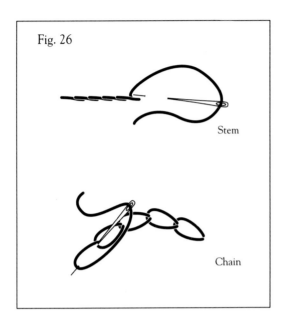

Fig. 26

Stem

Chain

Embellishment

When a unit of four blocks has been appliqued and embroidered, press lightly with a steam iron from the back side, then sew on the sequins and beads as indicated on the patterns. MY MOTHER TAUGHT ME TO SEW is embellished with flat, unfaceted ivory sequins, secured by pearl seed beads. Each one is sewn on twice using beading or quilting thread (Fig. 28). If your work is to be more functional than decorative, you might prefer to use very small baby buttons, which are more durable and can be washed or dry cleaned.

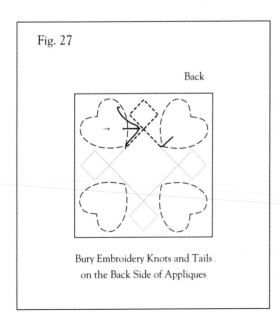

Fig. 27

Back

Bury Embroidery Knots and Tails
on the Back Side of Appliques

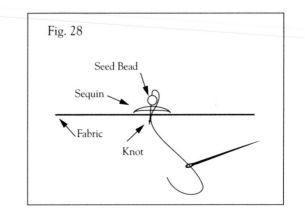

Fig. 28

Seed Bead

Sequin

Fabric

Knot

Separating the Blocks

When all the blocks have been completed for your project, use the original 6" x 6" template to make sure that each block is still perfectly square; make any adjustments needed. With a ruler, mark a ¼" seam allowance around each block and carefully cut the four blocks apart with scissors or a rotary cutter (Fig. 29).

Completing the Project

The blocks are now ready to be incorporated in your project. If you plan to join many blocks to make a quilt, arrange the separated blocks for a pleasant balance of shape, color and pattern. It can be very helpful to tack a cotton sheet or piece of muslin to the wall and arrange the blocks on this rather than look at them at an angle on a table. After you decide on the placement, stitch the blocks together into rows with ¼" seams and press the seams all in one direction (Fig. 30). Pin the rows of blocks together, matching seams, and stitch the rows in the same manner.

Finish the project off in the method of your choice – and enjoy the results of your efforts!

Fig. 29

COMPLETED UNIT

¼" Seam Allowance Added

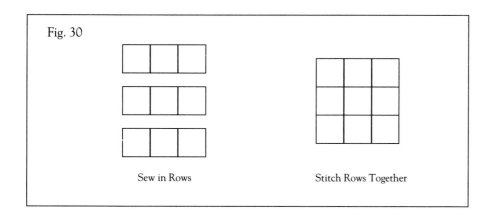

Fig. 30

Sew in Rows   Stitch Rows Together

Guide For 6" x 6" Squares

Use this square as a guide for cutting tracing paper for overlays (see "Overlays," pg. 11) and as a pattern for making a template for marking block overlays on background units (see "Templates," pg. 11).

BLOCK DESIGNS and PATTERNS

Full-Size Patterns for Fifty Designs

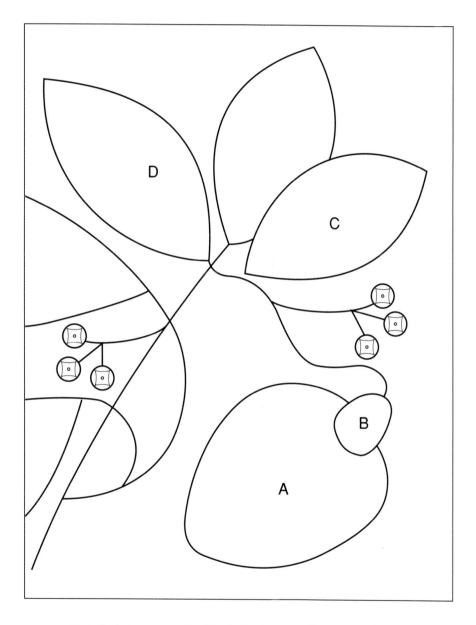

Detail of the pattern for Block Design #11 (See page 38).

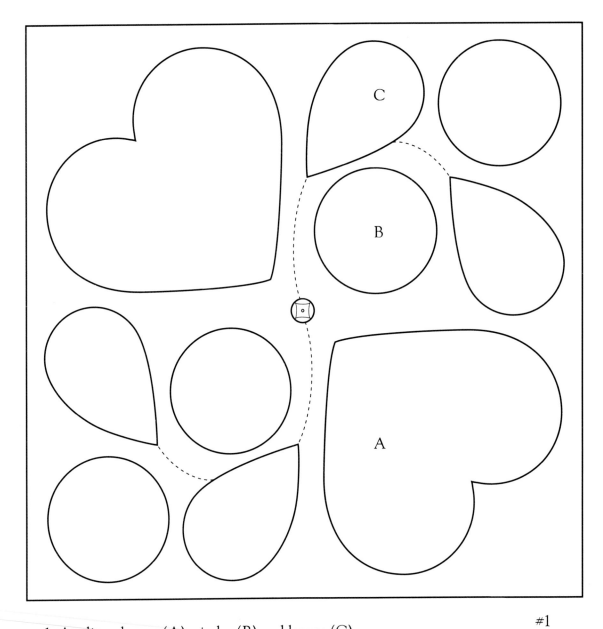

1. Applique hearts (A), circles (B) and leaves (C)
2. Mark embroidery lines (- - - - - -)
3. Embroider
4. Sew on sequins ((◦))

#1

1. Applique hearts (A)
2. Begin at 12 o'clock then 6, 9, and 3,
   and then fill in at 1, 4, 7, and 10

#2

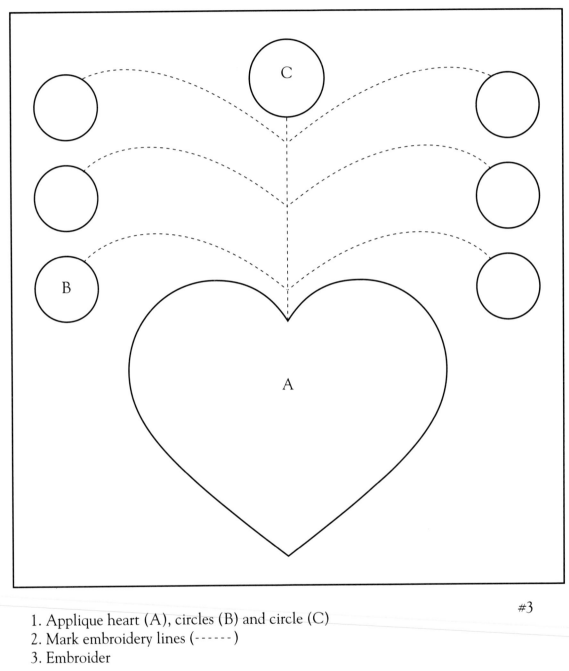

1. Applique heart (A), circles (B) and circle (C)
2. Mark embroidery lines (------)
3. Embroider

#3

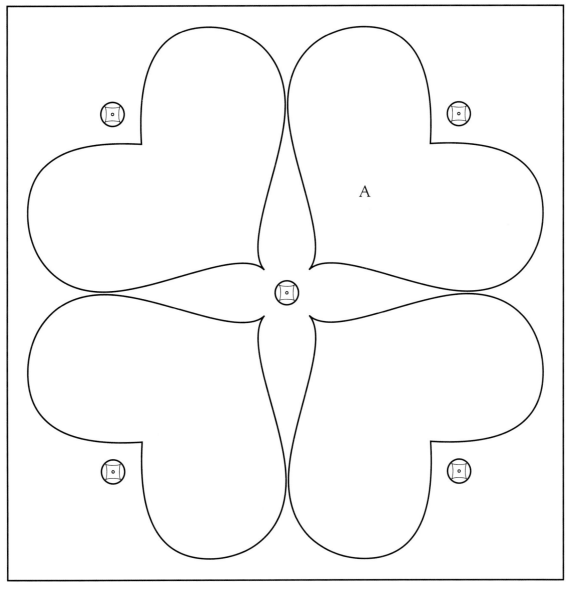

1. Applique hearts (A)
2. Sew on sequins ( )

#4

31

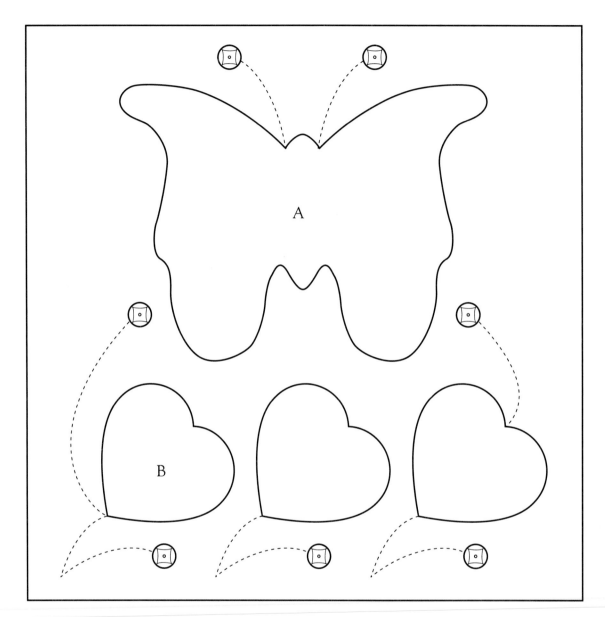

1. Applique butterfly (A) and hearts (B)
2. Mark embroidery lines (------)
3. Embroider
4. Sew on sequins (⊡)

#5

1. Applique baskets (A) and flowers (B)
2. Trim back of (B)
3. Applique circles (C)

#6

33

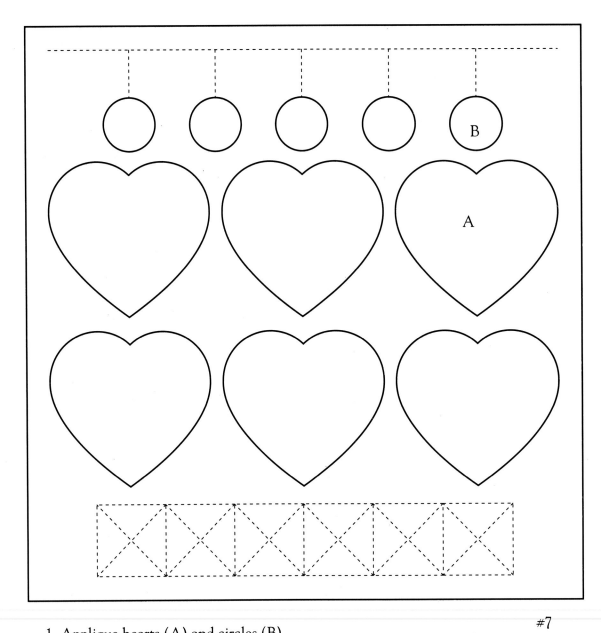

1. Applique hearts (A) and circles (B)
2. Mark embroidery lines (------)
3. Embroider

#7

34

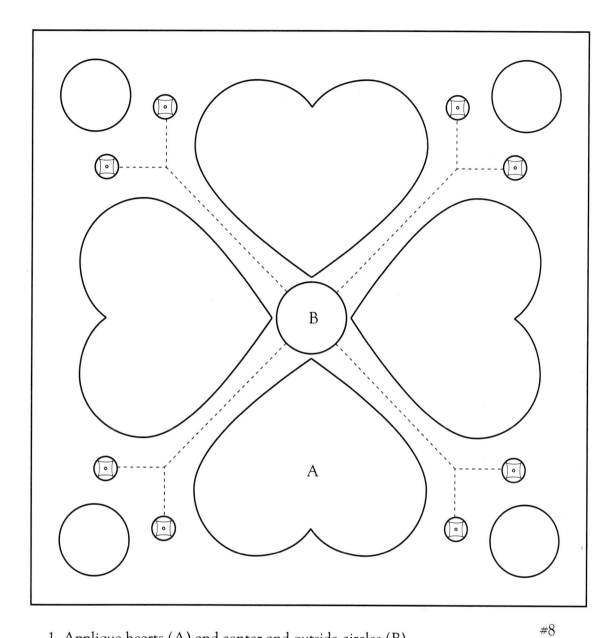

1. Applique hearts (A) and center and outside circles (B)
2. Mark embroidery lines (- - - - -)
3. Embroider
4. Sew on sequins (⊡)

#8

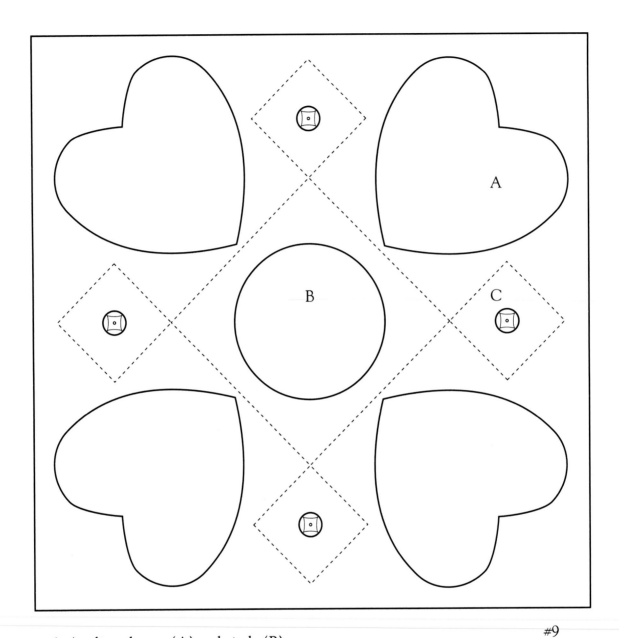

1. Applique hearts (A) and circle (B)
2. Square (C) can be appliqued or used as a template to aid in
   marking embroidery lines (------)
   Draw embroidery lines connecting squares, as in pattern
3. Embroider
4. Sew on sequins (⊡)

36

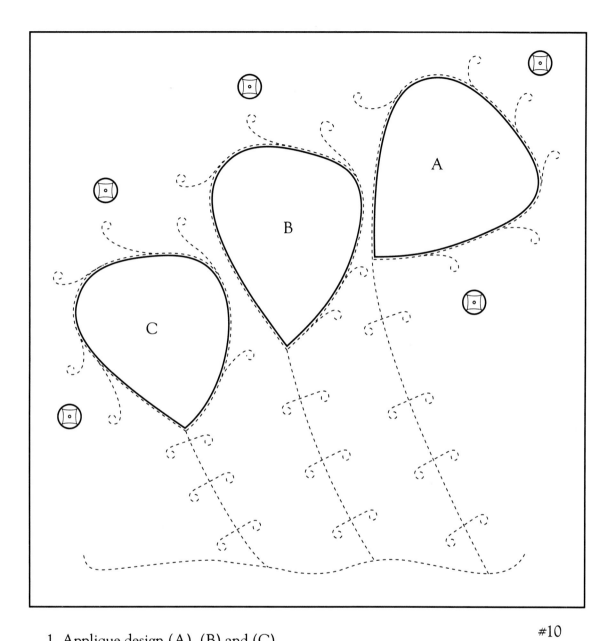

#10

1. Applique design (A), (B) and (C)
2. Mark embroidery lines (------)
3. Embroider on lines and around appliqued pieces
4. Sew on sequins (⊡)

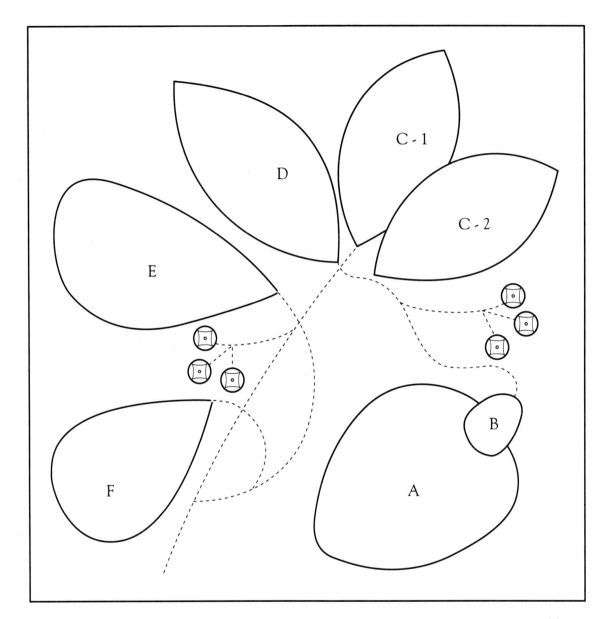

1. Applique pieces (A) through (F)
2. Mark embroidery lines (- - - - - -)
3. Embroider
4. Sew on sequins ( )

#11

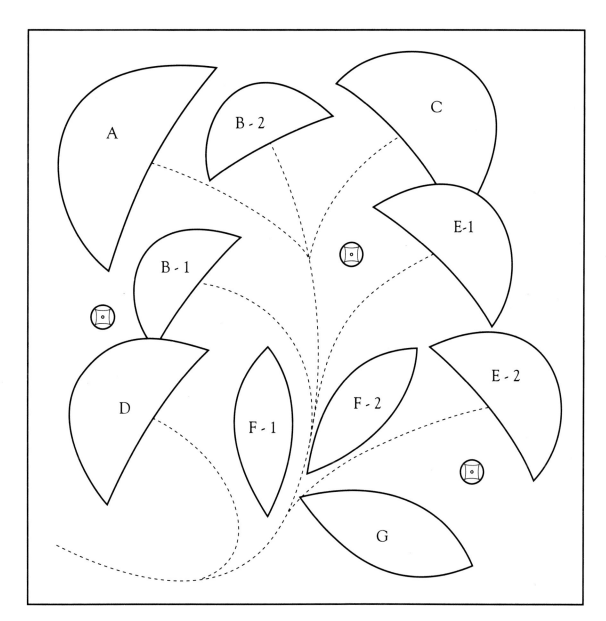

1. Applique pieces (A) through (G)
2. Mark embroidery lines (------)
3. Embroider
4. Sew on sequins (⊡)

#12

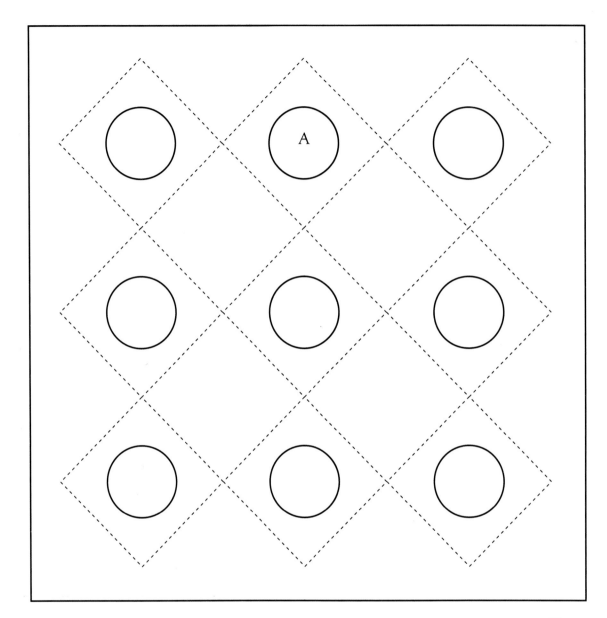

1. Applique circles (A)
2. Mark embroidery lines (------)
3. Embroider

#13

#14

1. Applique pieces (A) through (I)
2. Mark embroidery lines (------)
3. Embroider
4. Sew on sequins ()

41

1. Applique leaves (A) and (B), hearts (C) and circle (D)
2. Mark embroidery lines (------)
3. Embroider
   Also embroider outside of circle (D) and rays out from it
4. Sew on sequins (⊡)

#15

#16

1. Applique hands (A) and hearts (B)
2. Embroider initials and/or date in center, between the hands

1. Applique shape (A) Trim back
2. Applique heart (B) Trim back
3. Make template of zigzag border and mark embroidery lines (------)
4. Embroider border
5. Sew on sequins ()

#17

44

1. Applique gingerbread men (A), heart (B), tulips (C),
   and small hearts (D)
2. Mark embroidery lines (------)
3. Embroider
4. Sew on sequins (⊡)

#18

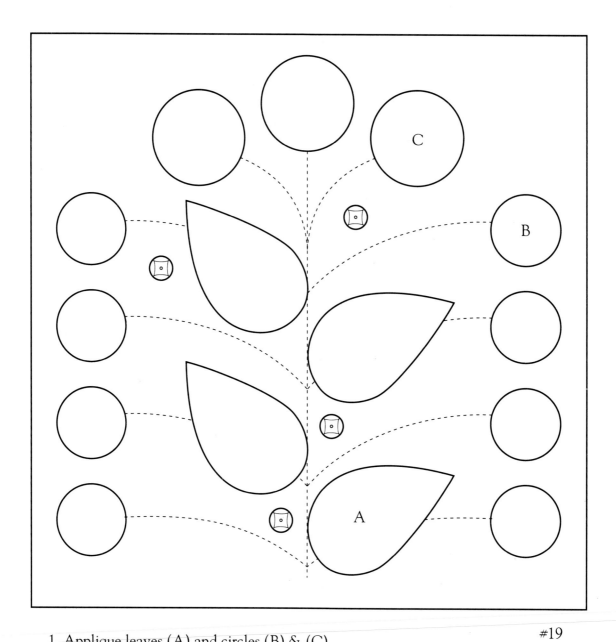

1. Applique leaves (A) and circles (B) & (C)
2. Mark embroidery lines (------)
3. Embroider
4. Sew on sequins ( )

#19

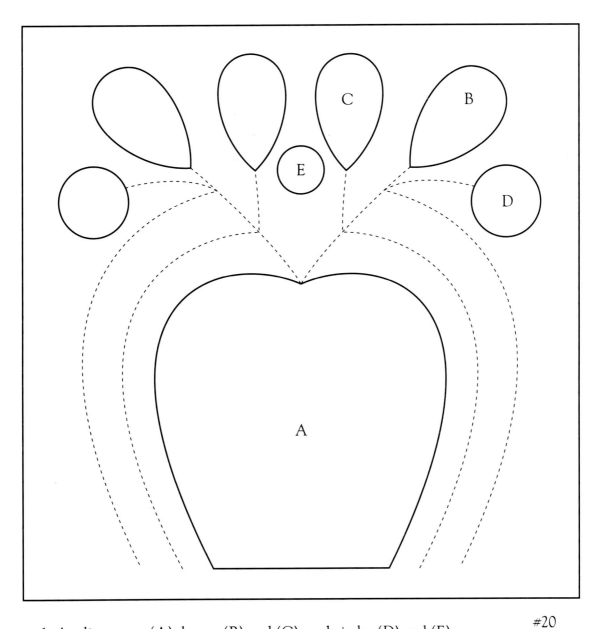

1. Applique vase (A), leaves (B) and (C), and circles (D) and (E)
2. Mark embroidery lines (------)
   It may help to make a template of the curves
   to get them symetrical on both sides of the vase
3. Embroider

#20

1. Applique basket (A), hearts (B) and tulips (C)
2. Mark embroidery lines (------)
3. Embroider
4. Sew on sequins ()

#21

1. Applique heart (A) Trim back
2. Applique heart (B) Trim back
3. Applique flower (C) on top of large hearts, center (D) and small hearts (E)
4. Mark embroidery lines (- - - - - -)
5. Embroider
6. Sew on sequins (⊡)

#22

1. Applique hand (A) Trim back
2. Applique hearts (B) and tulips (C)
3. Mark embroidery lines (------)
4. Embroider

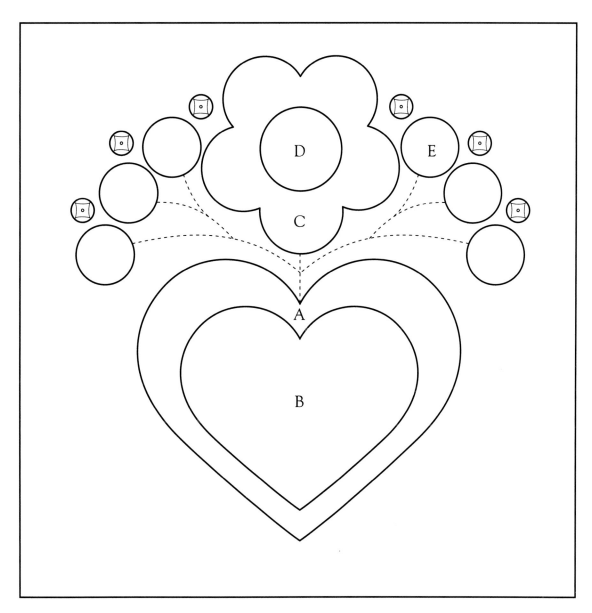

#24

1. Applique heart (A) Trim back
2. Applique heart (B)
3. Applique flower (C) Trim back
4. Applique center (D) and circles (E)
5. Mark embroidery lines (------)
6. Embroider
7. Sew on sequins (⊙)

1. Applique flower (A) Trim back
2. Applique flower (B) Trim back
3. Applique center (C), leaves (D), (E) and (F), and circles (G)
4. Mark embroidery lines (------)
5. Embroider
6. Sew on sequins (⊡)

#25

1. Applique hearts (A)
2. Mark embroidery lines (------)
3. Embroider

#26

1. Mark embroidery lines (------)
2. Embroider
3. Applique Cat (A)

#27

1. Applique leaves (A) and (B) and star flowers (C)
2. Mark embroidery lines (- - - - - -)
3. Embroider

#28

55

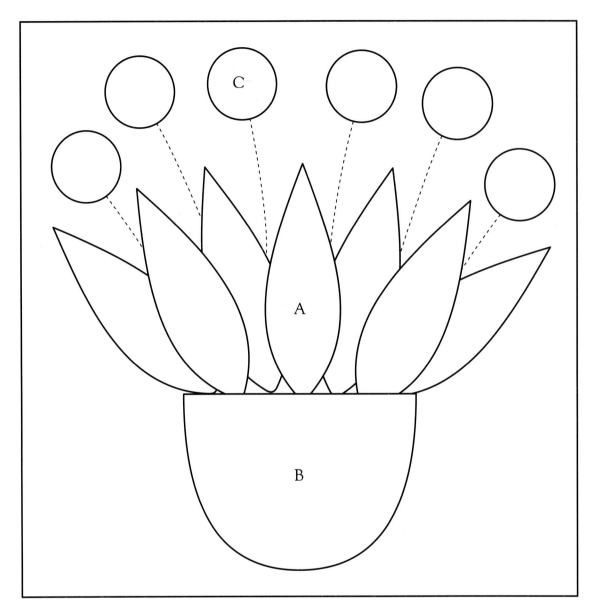

1. Applique 4 leaves (A) as back row and then 3 as front row as in pattern diagram. Lower edges may be left raw where they will be covered by bowl
2. Applique bowl (B) and flowers (C)
3. Mark embroidery lines (------)
4. Embroider

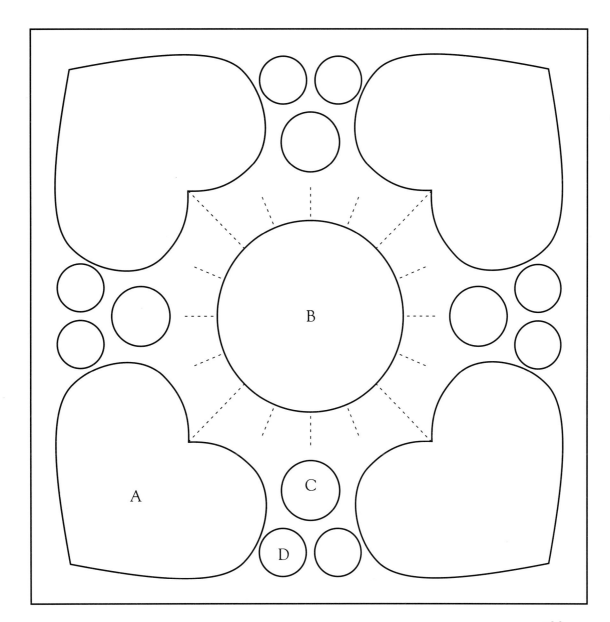

1. Applique hearts (A) and circles (B), (C), and (D)
2. Mark embroidery lines (------)
3. Embroider
4. Sew seed beads on ends of the spokes (optional)

#30

57

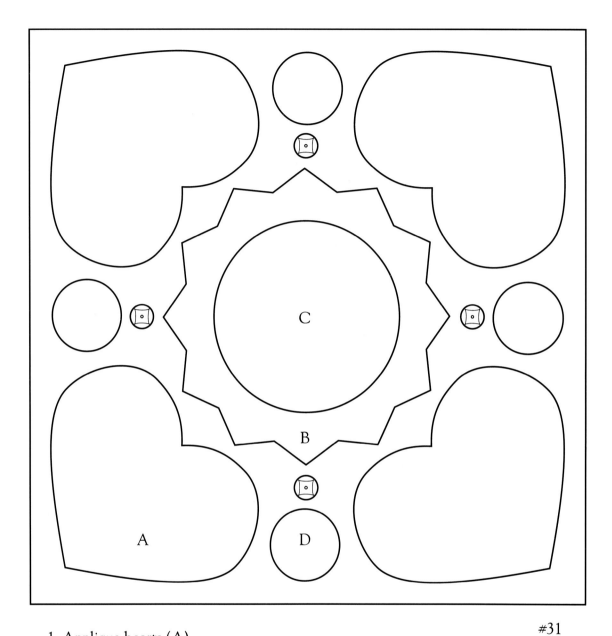

1. Applique hearts (A)
2. Applique shape (B)
   Trim back
   These points are a double fold, not a triple fold
3. Applique circle (C) and circles (D)
4. Sew on sequins ( )

#31

1. Applique hearts (A), flowers (B) and leaves (C)
2. Mark embroidery lines (------)
3. Embroider
4. Sew on sequin (⊙)

#32

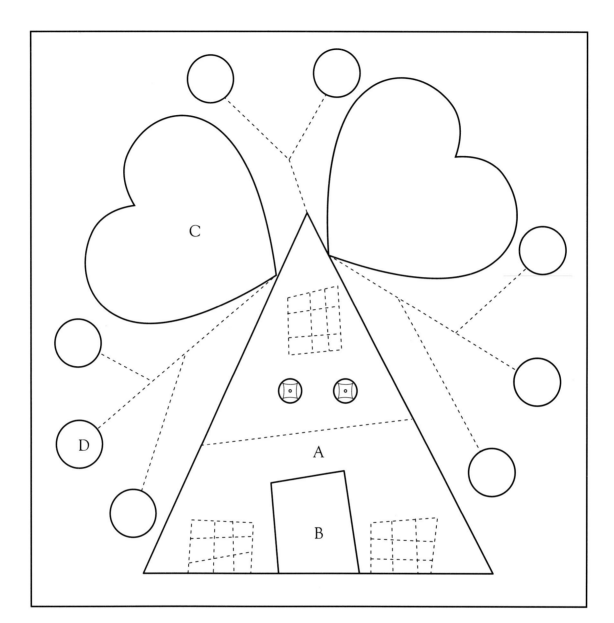

1. Applique house (A) Trim back
2. Applique door (B), hearts (C) and circles (D)
3. Mark embroidery lines (------)
4. Embroider
5. Sew on sequins (⬡)

#33

60

1. Applique leaf (A) Leave edges raw that will be covered by (B) and (D)
2. Applique leaf (B) Leave edges raw that will be covered by (C) and (D)
3. Applique leaf (C) Leave edges raw that will be covered by (D)
4. Applique pitcher (D) Trim back
5. Applique heart (E)
6. Applique flower piece (F) Leave edges raw that will be covered by (G)
7. Applique flower (G)
8. Mark embroidery lines (------)
9. Embroider
10. Sew on sequins (⊡)

#34

1. Applique tulips (A) and hearts (B) and (C)
2. Mark embroidery lines (------)
3. Embroider
4. Sew on sequins ()

#35

1. Applique flower (A)
   Leave edges raw where (B) will overlap
2. Applique flower base (B) and leaves (C), (D), and (E)
3. Mark embroidery lines (------)
4. Embroider
5. Sew on sequins (⊡)

#36

1. Applique flower piece (A)
   Leave edges raw where they will be covered by (B)
2. Applique flower piece (B) and leaves (C), (D), (E) & (F)
3. Mark embroidery lines (------)
4. Embroider
5. Sew on sequins (⊡)

#37

1. Applique leaves (A)
   Leave lower edge raw where it will be covered by (B)
2. Applique circle (B) Trim back
3. Applique circles (C) & (D)
4. Mark embroidery lines (------)
5. Embroider
6. Sew on sequins ( )

#38

1. Applique petals (A)
   Stitch petals at 12, 5, and 7 o'clock then overlap with petals at 10 and 2
2. Applique leaves (B), tulips (C), heart (D) and flower (E) Trim back of (E)
3. Applique circle (F)
4. Mark embroidery lines (------)
5. Embroider
6. Sew on sequin ( )

#39

66

#40

1. Applique (A) Trim back
2. Applique (B) Trim back
3. Applique (C) Trim back
4. Applique petals (D)
   Stitch petals at 12, 4 and 8 o'clock
   Then fill in with petals at 10, 2 and 6
   Leave inside edges raw where they will be covered by (E)
5. Applique (E)
6. Sew on sequins (⊡)

67

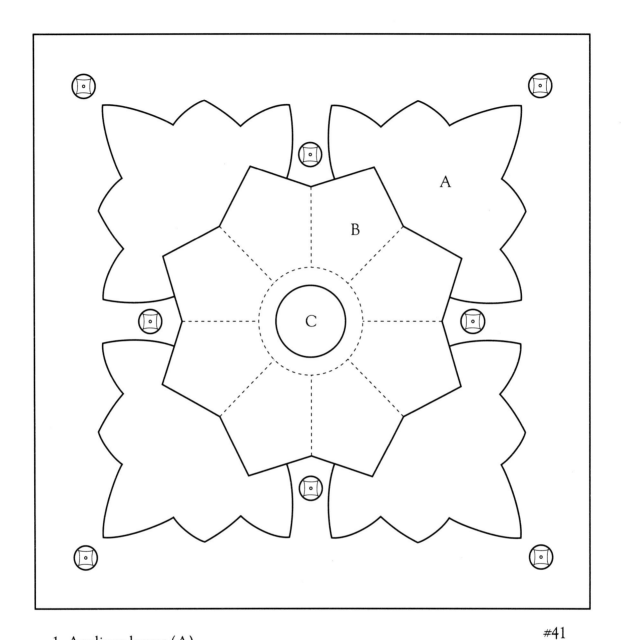

#41

1. Applique leaves (A)
   Leave edges raw where they will be covered by (B)
2. Applique (B)
   These points are double, not triple fold. Trim back.
3. Applique circle (C)
4. Mark embroidery lines (------)
5. Embroider
6. Sew on sequins (⊡)

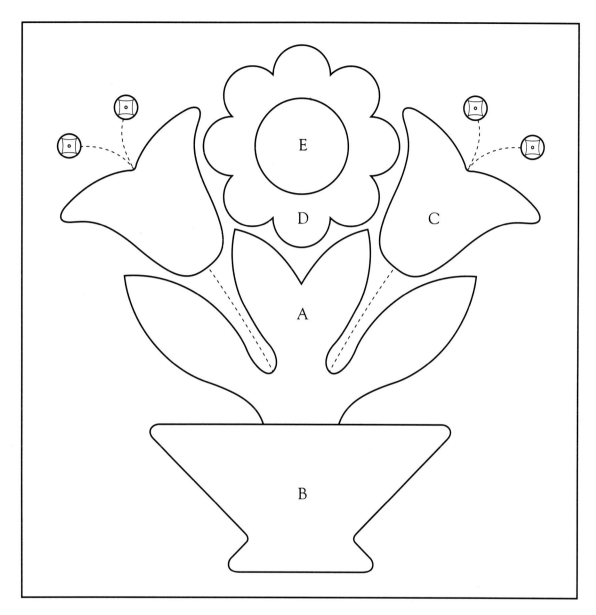

1. Applique leaves (A) using cut-as-you-go technique
   Leave lower edge raw where it will be covered by (B)
2. Applique vase (B), Tulips (C), and flower (D)
   Trim back of (D)
3. Applique circle (E)
4. Mark embroidery lines (------)
5. Embroider
6. Sew on sequins (⊡)

#42

69

1. Applique background (A) Trim back
2. Applique heart (B) Trim back
3. Mark embroidery lines (------)
4. Embroider
5. Sew on sequins ()

#43

1. Applique flower (A) using cut-as-you-go technique
   Trim back
2. Applique flower (B) Trim back
3. Applique circle (C)
4. Mark embroidery lines (- - - - -)
5. Embroider
6. Sew on sequins ( )

#45

1. Applique leaves (A) using cut-as-you-go technique
2. Applique flowers (B)
3. Mark embroidery lines (------)
4. Embroider

#46

1. Applique buds (A)
   Leave edge raw where they will be covered by (B)
2. Applique flowers (B)
   Leave edges raw where they will be covered by (C)
3. Applique flower (C) Trim back
4. Applique circle (D)
5. Applique leaves (E)
6. Mark embroidery lines (------)
7. Embroider
8. Sew on sequins (⊙)

1. Applique shape (A) using cut-as-you-go technique
   Trim back
2. Applique hearts (B) and center (C)
3. Sew on sequins ()

#47

#48

1. Applique shape (A)
   Leave edges raw where they will be covered by hearts (B)
2. Applique hearts (B) and petals (C) at 2, 4, 7, and 10 o'clock
   Overlap with petals at 12, 3, 6, &9
   Leave edges raw where they will be covered by circle (D)
3. Applique circle (D)
4. Sew on sequins (⊙)

#49

1. Applique leaves (A)
   Leave edges raw where they will be covered by (B)
2. Applique flower (B) Trim back
3. Applique circle (C) and corners (D)
   Optional: Shape (D) may be embroidered
4. Mark embroidery lines (------)
5. Embroider
6. Sew on sequins (⊡)

1. Mark embroidery lines (------)
2. Embroider
3. Applique petals (A)
4. Sew on sequins ()

#50

Four block designs are featured in this pillow by Susan Sternlieb, one of the author's students.

The same four appliqued blocks are also used in this pillow by the author.

Wool vest with cotton applique squares embroidered in gold metallic thread; black crystal bead accents.

SAMPLE PROJECTS

The author's *Floradora* wall quilt, which includes
many designs featured in this book.
Photo by Jerry De Felice.

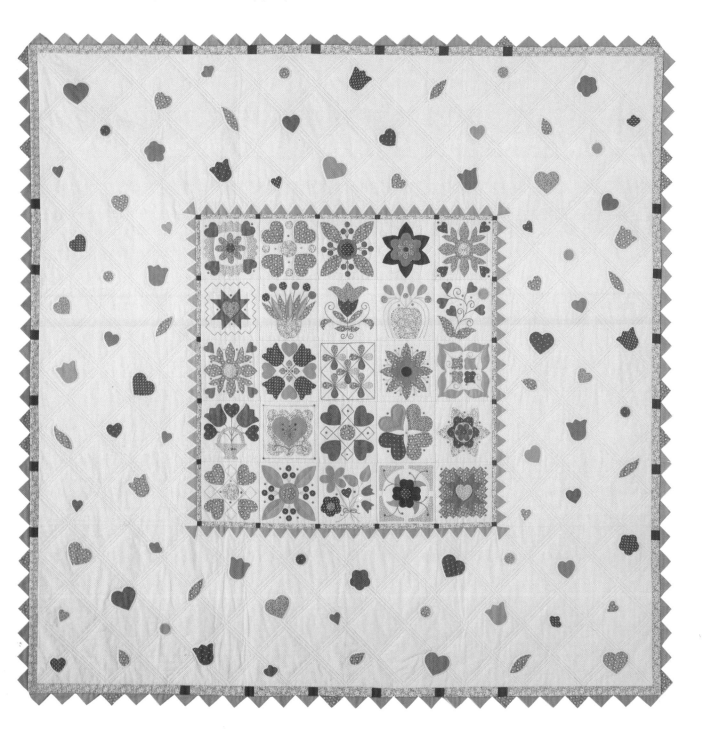